A Victory For Jamie

The Story of
Greg Norman and Jamie Hutton

Ronald McDonald
Children's Charities ®

Established in memory of Ray A. Kroc

All profits will be donated to Ronald McDonald Children's Charities in the name of Jamie Hutton.

ISBN 0-9615344-4-3

©1989 Great White Shark Enterprises, Inc.

Published by International Merchandising Corporation
One Erieview Plaza, Cleveland, Ohio 44114

Printed in the United States of America

A Victory For Jamie

The Story of
Greg Norman and Jamie Hutton

Lawrence Levy
Gordon S. White, Jr.

Foreword

Covering the golf tour around the world as a photographer over the past ten years has given me the opportunity of meeting many people and visiting many places. It has also made me feel the tremendous varying degrees of emotions that this game produces.

What I experienced on Hilton Head Island at the 1988 Heritage was something that was both unique and very special.

When Greg and I first met Jamie at breakfast that Friday morning, we both felt that we wanted to do as much as we could to make his dream come true.

In Jamie I saw something of myself when I was that age. A love of the game and those that play it at the highest level and the thrills of following your man.

Greg showed the world something that I have known for sometime. He is the most gifted of golfers and the most genuine and generous of people. He is a class act. He felt that his victory was inspired by Jamie and his gift of the trophy was something that touched all of us that watched the closing ceremony.

This book will tell the story in words and pictures of that weekend. It may sound like a fairy tale, but that is exactly what it turned out to be.

I feel very honored and priviledged to have been a part of this story and to have spent the time with Jamie. The experience has taught me a lot about courage, determination and winning, but most of all it made me realize that dreams can come true.

Lawrence Levy

Greg Norman was uneasy as he stood over the six-foot putt on the final hole of the MCI Heritage Classic. He had stood over hundreds of clutch putts, but this one felt different. Ordinarily, nothing could disturb his steely discipline. But this time an alien feeling had intruded.

It was an inspiration, not a distraction.

Looking down at the ball for the last time, Norman understood. It was then that he fully realized how powerful an impact the desperately ill boy had had on him.

"This one is for Jamie," Norman said to himself.

And coolly, he drew the putter back, stroked firmly, and the ball rolled true and dropped. Norman did more than win a golf tournament for himself that day. He rewarded the faith of a young, new friend who had a great fighting spirit, and who idolized him.

Jamie knew all about Greg's favorite things and brought him a shark headcover for his driver and a Boston Celtics cap.

At the Harbour Town Golf Links on South Carolina's Hilton Head Island, fans caught glimpses of the frail-looking boy in the white golf cap that weekend in mid-April, 1988. Millions more saw him on television as the cameras zeroed in. His face was tense and his fingers were crossed. He was wishing, hoping, willing Norman to success.

This was Jamie — James Garfield Hutton, age 17, of Monona, Wisconsin.

"Never before, when I played golf," Norman said, "had my mind been on another thought than executing the stroke at hand, particularly with a shot as crucial as that. I knew if I made the putt, I had a good chance to win the golf tournament.

"But when I was lining up that last putt, and just about to take it back — believe it or not — all I kept saying to myself was, 'This one is for Jamie.' That was probably more pressure than I have ever put on myself — because I knew I would break the boy's heart if I missed it."

Norman made a furious charge that final day. He came from four strokes behind and shot a 66, and won by a stroke. It was a triumph that did much more than add another championship to his great career. It was a victory that literally made a boy's dream come true at the end of the most thrilling week of his difficult life.

Jamie Hutton had the unfortunate distinction of being, as doctors described it, a thirty million-to-one shot. Jamie, the youngest of three children, had suffered from Crohn's disease since he was seven. He struggled for years with this chronic intestinal inflammation. Then in February, 1988, just some two months before the Heritage Classic, doctors at the University of Wisconsin Medical Center in Madison found that he also had leukemia. Thirty million-to-one, they said, that anyone could have two unrelated diseases. As one doctor put it, "It is as unlikely as being struck by lightning while involved in an

Greg introduced Jamie to the stars of the PGA Tour including Sandy Lyle, Tom Watson, Peter Jacobsen and (following page) Paul Azinger, Curtis Strange, Bernhard Langer and Lanny Wadkins.

automobile accident."

Mrs. Garnett Hutton, Jamie's mother and closest friend, remembers well the day they learned there was no doubt about the leukemia. She also remembers that it was Jamie who found the strength.

"We cried, just Jamie and I, in the apartment," she said. "Then Jamie stopped, and he said, 'OK, Mom. Now we know I have it. We can deal with it.'"

Although he was limited by his illnesses, Jamie was a normal kid at Monona High School. He liked fried chicken and Tom Hanks movies. He would hero-worship athletes and laugh with friends, smile bashfully around girls and probably fall in love with every second or third one he met. But

in his way, he was tougher than the rest. He had to be. He never stopped smiling, and he never stopped fighting those invaders that had hospitalized him so much of his young life.

Jamie became friends with Greg Norman through a way that is relatively new on the American scene — organizations that try to make wishes come true for youngsters suffering from lengthy or threatening illnesses. In Jamie's home area, it was Thursday's Child. Kids may wish to take a trip to Disney World or the Grand Canyon, or to ride a horse or swim in the ocean. For Jamie, it was to meet Greg Norman.

An avid sports fan, Jamie had a particu-

lar interest in National Basketball Association superstars Michael Jordan, of the Chicago Bulls, and Larry Bird, of the Boston Celtics. He hung their autographed pictures in his bedroom. But just a glance around the room made it clear that the big, stark-blond Australian swashbuckler was his main man. The life-sized poster, pictures, and magazines covered the walls and bookcases — a Greg Norman shrine in Monona, Wisconsin.

For Norman, back in August, 1987, Jamie Hutton was nothing more than just a name. Jamie's mother had written, saying that Jamie was sick and would appreciate an autographed photo. But Norman had no way of knowing just how much he meant to this young fan in Wisconsin. When Thursday's Child asked Jamie what he was wishing for, he said, "I want to go and watch Greg Norman play in a golf tournament . . ."

If you're going to wish, wish big. Jamie added a provision at the end of that sentence. It was: ". . . and win."

The first part was easy enough. Thursday's Child could get Jamie to a golf tournament, put him up for a couple of nights in a hotel with his mother, and get him home. Jamie had no trouble picking a tournament. A call to Norman's management organization, International Management

Reporters and photographers became interested in Jamie, who obliged them with a short interview before going to watch Greg play his second round.

16

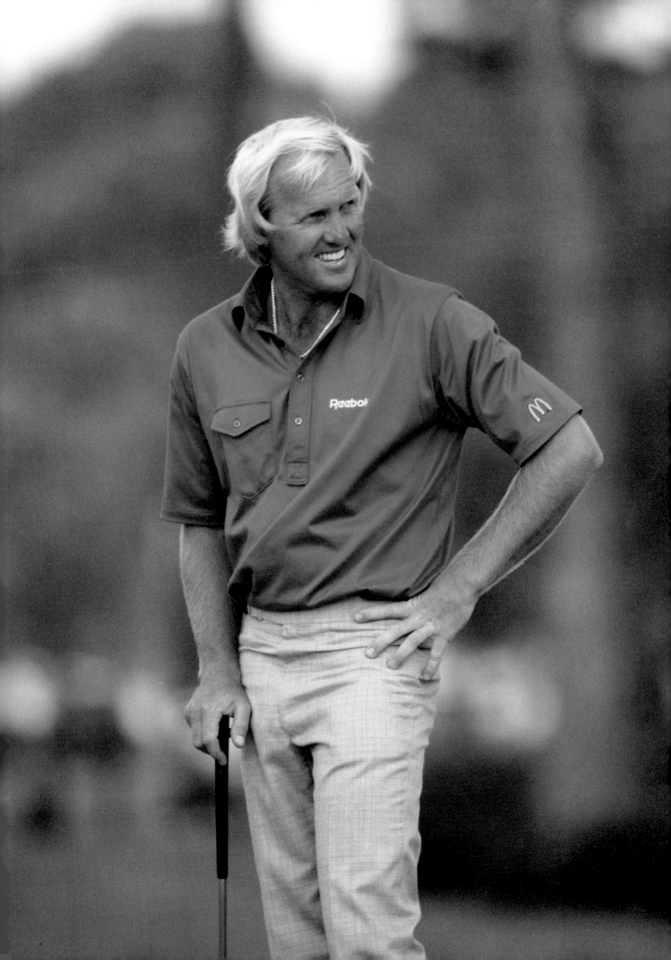

Group, in Cleveland, got him the playing schedule. As for winning? Well, Thursday's Child would have to defer to Mr. Norman for that.

Jamie knew just about everything there was to know about Greg Norman. It was all there in the articles he had cut out and pasted in his scrapbook. He knew, for example, that Greg was a big Boston Celtics fan and that he, like Jamie himself, rooted hard for Larry Bird. So when Thursday's Child informed the Huttons that arrangements had been completed for the plane trip from Madison to Hilton Head, Jamie went on a little shopping trip. He had run short of cash buying a golf club head cover in the shape of a white shark, so with his mother's permission, he used her credit card to buy a Boston Celtics cap.

By this time, Norman had been told of Jamie's wish, and he was informed that the Huttons would arrive during the Heritage Classic.

"We just figured he would fly in that day and fly out the next day or so," Norman said.

That was also about the way Jamie and his mother had it figured. They had tickets to get to Hilton Head on Thursday evening and to fly out Sunday morning. But no one could have foreseen how completely Jamie was to affect Norman.

Jamie and his mother reached Hilton Head later than expected Thursday. Jamie couldn't wait for the next day. He telephoned Norman that night, about 11 o'clock.

"I was asleep when he called to say he was there," Norman said, chuckling. "So we set a date to have breakfast the next

Greg kept a watch for Jamie during his second round and for the rest of the tournament.

morning before the round."

Things were happening fast for the young man. And Mrs. Hutton was nervous when they walked into the restaurant for breakfast. They were about to meet that autographed photo hanging on the wall, but real and bigger than life.

"We were super-excited," Jamie said. "Mom and I arrived early so we could watch for him. When we told the waitress we were waiting for Mr. Norman, she said he was already seated, but that she would tell him. In a few minutes, he walked over to our table with a bowl of corn flakes. I couldn't believe he eats corn flakes! He was like a normal person."

Greg Norman, who is by all standards a superstar, is also as likeable a regular guy as one can find in the world of professional sports. There are no airs about the Australian. He loves his trade and enjoys people. Far from being a loner, as some athletes become in the face of a curious public, Norman handles himself with rare comfort and ease. He laughs easily and trades jibes with anyone. If he likes you, you know it. And if he doesn't, you probably won't ever realize it.

Norman is 6-foot-2 and broad-shouldered, and he stands out in any crowd because of that thick, flaxen mane. To those who know him best, he is both a gentle man and a gentleman. He also has that extra-special sensitivity to the plight of youngsters that comes with being a parent.

Laura Norman, a native of Perth Amboy, New Jersey, speaks of her husband as "a man who is most comfortable being with men and doing men's things, such as fishing. But no one could be a gentler or better father." The Normans, who live in Florida, have a daughter and a son — Morgan-Leigh and Gregory.

That first meeting of Jamie and Norman seemed more like a reunion of old friends

than an introduction of two strangers. Jamie, the hero-worshipping sick boy, could have been awed into total and uncomfortable silence. But though he was a hero-worshipper, he was not a fawner. Norman, the hero, might have been stuffy and put out. But Greg is Greg.

"Those two hit it off so well when they first met that I wasn't nervous once I sat down," said Mrs. Hutton. "Sure, Jamie and I were surprised how real he was. Do we ever really know what kind of person our heroes are until we actually meet them?"

Breakfast included a brief, informal ceremony. Jamie presented Greg with the Boston Celtics cap.

Jamie was going through a series of thrilling firsts in his young life. He had just flown in a plane for the first time, and a few hours later he had met his hero. After a relaxed breakfast, Greg and Jamie strolled out to the beach. Jamie pulled up short and gawked. There was the Atlantic Ocean.

"I'll never forget his first words — 'My God, it's so big!'" Norman said. "Then I realized he had never seen the ocean before. Heck, he had never seen a palm tree before, either."

The ocean visit was brief. Norman had some business to attend to Friday afternoon. He and Paul Azinger had a spirited duel in the first round. Norman scored four birdies on the front nine, and Azinger birdied the last three holes, and they tied for the lead with six-under-par 65s.

At the practice tee before the second round, Norman received his other gift, the shark head cover, and he introduced Jamie to other big names in golf — Azinger, Curtis Strange, Sandy Lyle, Tom Watson, Lanny Wadkins and others.

"Tom was great with Jamie," Norman said. "Then Jamie, who has a real wit, was speaking with Lanny and wished him good luck. 'But I hope you come in second,' he told Lanny. We all broke up over that."

Coincidentally, Curtis Strange also had a young guest who was suffering from leukemia. Michael House, of Virginia Beach, Virginia, had come to the Heritage Classic through the Make A Wish Foundation, an organization that does much the same things as Thursday's Child.

"It's the least you can do," said Strange, "especially when you have two healthy kids of your own at home." Strange is the father of two boys, Tom and David.

Strange introduced Michael to Tom Watson, and found him, like Norman, more than willing to greet the young man.

"Tom was just super with Mike," Strange said. "I thought maybe he would talk with him for a couple of minutes after I introduced them. Forty-five minutes later, Tom had to break it off to go to the first tee for his round."

On the practice green, Jamie was tossing balls back to Greg. He couldn't resist kicking a few in with his heels. Then, as they were leaving, he kicked one in from 40 feet. This did not go unnoticed by Lawrence Levy, a British golf photographer and a close friend of Norman's. Levy is forever on the golf scene somewhere. He's the photographer whose trademark is — oddly enough for an Englishman — a New York Yankees baseball cap. If that's not odd enough, how about Jamie's characterization of his new-found British friend: "An all-American tough guy."

Now, this might not stand up with fans of the occult, but Levy interpreted Jamie's long kick as something of a premonition, and he mentioned it to Norman at dinner that evening. That did it. Norman was already taken with the kid. Now he and Levy would see to it that Jamie would have a great weekend.

But before that, the day — the second

round — had gone strangely for Norman. Something was gnawing at him. He didn't know it at the time, of course, but it was only a sample of what was in store for him when he stood over that putt on that final green of the tournament two days later.

"The hardest part for me was the first five holes I played Friday," Norman said. "I wasn't zeroed in on the whole deal. I was thinking of Jamie walking around, and that's when the thing hit me pretty strongly.

"He's such a like- able guy, and think- ing what could have happened to him hit hard. His life was not going to be a long, normal life. I was thinking — and it took me six holes to get back down to the game.

"And all of this after only knowing him for four or five hours. When we sat down for two hours at breakfast and walked the beach, he showed no signs of being despondent. He's so open about it all that it just strikes you — those of us lucky enough to be healthy."

While Greg was struggling with his game — those disquieting thoughts were com- peting for his attention — Jamie was walk- ing the course to watch his hero play. The first part of his wish had come true.

Jamie did not lack for company during the round. Lawrence Levy, the photo- grapher, had taken Jamie under his wing

as they followed Norman around the course.

The day went by, with Norman slipping just a bit as he lost the lead after two rounds. He had opened the day with bir- dies on the first two holes, then bogeys on the next two. "There's nothing worse than a start like that," he said. He finished strong, with birdies on the sixteenth and eighteenth for a 69 and a 134 total. He was one shot off the pace — nothing much to worry about and a good position to be in halfway through any tournament.

The exciting day took its toll on Jamie. He was too tired to join Norman and Levy for dinner, so he and his mother returned to their hotel room. There was — they thought — just one more big day ahead before they had to return to Wisconsin. And Jamie wanted to cram in every mo- ment he could with Greg on Saturday, the day of the third round.

Mrs. Hutton re- members that Friday night so well.

"We were going to bed early because Jamie was so tired," she said. "Just as I was about to turn off the light, Jamie said, 'Mom, don't turn off the light yet. I want you to look at me. You are looking at a boy who just had the greatest day of his life.'" Jamie was wrong.

There were bigger surprises in store.

Jamie helped out Greg on the practice green as he studied the Shark's putting style.

The courageous young man didn't know it, but he had worked his way into the heart of the Australian golfer. Jamie began to discover this Saturday morning.

"Do you really have to fly back Sunday morning?" Norman asked Jamie and his mother at breakfast.

It would seem so. "I have to go to the hospital Monday to begin tests for a marrow transplant," Jamie explained. That meant he and his mother would have to drive to Savannah, Georgia, some 30 miles away, catch the flight, and change planes in Atlanta and again in Chicago to get back to Madison.

Norman and Levy had a better idea.

"We've gotten a private plane for you," Norman said. "Think you can change plans and catch it after the Sunday round? It will fly you right from Hilton Head to Madison. Give it some thought."

Jamie did. About 20 seconds' worth.

"We can change our plans," he said.

It was done. Norman and Levy had chartered a private plane that would take the Huttons nonstop from Hilton Head to Madison. The young man who thought he had just had the greatest day of his life was about to top it.

Golf was put aside for a while that Saturday morning. Norman arranged for Jamie and his mother to cruise the Island Waterway aboard a power boat owned by the Melrose Corporation. Jamie sat at the bow, shooting pictures of the playful porpoises frolicking through the wakes of passing boats. Then the skipper let Jamie take the helm for a while. The dream was growing by leaps and bounds.

"This wasn't just about golf and games," Norman said. "It was about life. He was getting to me as if he was family."

It was time to leave the boat, finally. Norman had to tee off, and Jamie wanted to be with him.

"To miss today's round," Jamie said, "would be like leaving the World Series in the last inning, score tied and the bases loaded."

Levy decided that a crowded gallery was no place for someone to be fighting for a view of his hero. He arranged for Jamie to accompany him inside the gallery ropes and even gave him some camera equipment to carry, just for a touch of propriety. By this time, practically everyone in the gallery, and all the writers and photographers, knew about that kid who was trudging the course in Norman's wake. Reporters began asking Jamie questions.

"Lawrence is the best golf photographer in the world," Jamie told one.

"Lawrence must have told you that," the reporter cracked.

"No sir," Jamie said, straight-faced. "Mr. Norman told me."

One reporter was interviewing Jamie,

After Greg's round on Saturday, the two of them watched the rest of the action by the 18th green and talked with CBS commentator Steve Melnyk.

and asked how he and Norman and Levy were getting on.

"It's so neat!" Jamie said. "They are so popular, and everyone would love to meet them. I not only met them, we are friends. They treat me like a normal kid. They don't feel sorry for me because I'm sick."

Jamie came away with another photo for his bedroom wall — one he took himself, thanks to Levy. "He let me take one picture, and he sent me a copy of it right away," Jamie said. "It's from behind the eighteenth tee, and Greg is hitting, with the lighthouse in the background. It turned out

Jamie got the lesson of a lifetime on the practice ground Saturday after play.

just wonderful."

In the third round, Norman shot a par 71 — "No putts," he explained — ordinarily a good score at Harbour Town. But these were not ordinary circumstances. The tournament was heating up. There was speculation that someone would break the record of 14 under par for 72 holes. Norman had begun the day one shot off the lead, and now the 72 left him four shots off. Things did not look good for the second part of Jamie's wish.

And worse, Jamie was hurting. His knees and some other joints were tired and

aching from the exertions of walking the course a second day. That was approximately four miles each day, and Jamie wasn't used to it.

Jamie's mother had to rub down his legs Saturday night, to help ease the pain.

"I asked him if he was sure he wanted to walk the course again Sunday," she said. Sharing the pain with her son, and suffering one all her own, she told him that Norman would understand if he didn't walk on Sunday. She knew she was wasting her time.

"Of course he was going to walk with Greg Sunday," she said. "I knew it."

She watched her son closely. "Everytime I saw his smile," she said, "I thought, 'Thank you, Thursday's Child. Thank you for this opportunity.'"

Sunday, for Jamie, started with an introduction to yet another noted figure in golf, Ken Venturi, CBS golf analyst. Venturi took Jamie on a tour of the wonders and mysteries of the television complex. Meanwhile, Jamie's new buddy had to confront a mystery of his own.

Norman faced an awesome task that final round. A four-shot deficit was tough enough. That's part of golf. But Norman also had something else riding on every swing of the club — the hopes of an adoring boy who had his fingers crossed.

"He was there every time I walked off a green," Norman said. "I saw him and knew he was wishing for me to win. That's not the easiest thing to carry around when you're on the course."

Before the last two rounds, Norman spent some time on the practice tee giving Jamie pointers on the swing and the game. It was not merely a superficial exercise in paying attention to the young man. Norman knew Jamie hoped to be a good golfer some day. And now Jamie was privy to something every duffer dreams of — les-

sons from one of the world's greatest golfers. To Greg's surprise, he found an eager student with something of a natural talent.

"He has extremely fine eye-hand coordination," Norman said. "He is capable of striking the ball very well. His illness has kept him from growing much, so he is smaller than most boys his age. But he can handle himself in a well-coordinated fashion, and without these diseases, would undoubtedly be a good athlete.

"Oh, what we who are not ill have to be thankful for. That kept hitting me all week while Jamie was with us. The feeling will never leave me again in my life."

Norman wasn't the only teacher. He and Jamie discussed tactics before the last round, and it was Jamie's opinion that he might be a little more aggressive with his putting. Norman agreed. And the putts started rolling in.

Norman moved into the lead with birdies on the fifth, eighth, and tenth holes to go to twelve under par. A surprise was waiting for him when he stepped onto the fourteenth tee. "That was the first time," he said, "I knew I had the lead."

Few golfers are as dangerous as Norman in the final round. He is famed for strong finishes. He was even more dangerous this time, for Jamie's little fingers remained crossed on every shot, and the smile grew every time he nailed one at the flagstick. Even so, Norman needed a cushion — one more birdie. He figured his last real chance on the tough course was at No. 15. He saw the flag tucked in at the front left part of the green. It was a sitting duck. Norman's pitch stopped five feet from the hole. He had his birdie.

Finally, he came to No. 18, that beautiful links finale, a long, straight par-four that presents the golfer with a nerve-shredding problem. The bay is to the left, and for anyone trying to steer clear of it by hitting to the right, there are trees and an out-of-bounds. In short, the golfer must swallow and hit straight.

Norman crunched one far down the middle. But his approach shot came up just a little short of the green. He chipped on, and par was six feet away. If he holed the putt, David Frost, his pursuer, would have a hard time catching him.

"The whole dream was coming true," Jamie said after it was all over.

That final six feet — that's when it all hit Norman the hardest. But he handled it perfectly for a 66 and a 13-under-par total of 271. Then he and Jamie sat on his golf bag and waited as Frost, the last man on the course with a chance to catch him, played the final hole. Frost had to make a 20-foot birdie putt to tie Norman and force a playoff. He missed, and Norman had a one-stroke victory. There may never have been a happier man or boy on a golf course than Greg Norman and Jamie Hutton that afternoon. One thing was almost forgotten in the high feelings — it was Norman's first victory on the American tour in two years.

"I'm very excited about winning again," Norman said. "But I'm more excited for Jamie. He told me at breakfast this morning he wanted a 64 from me and for me to win. I didn't get the 64, but I got the win, and I guess that's OK. I'm not out here to be a hero. I just wanted to fulfill a wish for Jamie." And then he added: "I just want to thank Jamie. He showed me inspiration and courage."

But was Norman a hero?

"He is to me," Jamie said. "Everybody has heroes they pick up along the way.

Some people like movie stars. I just like Mr. Norman."

Norman found yet another way to mark their friendship. When he accepted the trophy, he turned to Jamie.

"I'd like you to have it and put it in your hospital room," he said. "This is your trophy."

It was the end of a draining weekend.

"Obviously, it was emotional at the eighteenth," Norman said. "In a way, it was like having your own son sitting there even through I had only known him for two days. He showed the emotion and love you experience in a family. Unless you go though it, you can't really feel it."

During the presentation ceremony, Jamie scanned the crowd of photographers and found the face he was searching for.

"I looked over at Lawrence and saw him wipe his eyes," he said. "I knew he was crying. That made me almost cry, too. It also made me realize how much I meant to him. It was for real."

Jamie also ended up in a red plaid jacket, the symbol of the Heritage Classic, that goes to the winner. Some thought Norman had given Jamie his. But this one fit Jamie fairly well. Greg's would have hung down at least to the boy's knees.

"A lady gave Jamie her jacket," Norman said, grinning. "So that's how he got the jacket that fit."

The crowded limousine to the Hilton Head airport carried a happy group — Jamie, his mother, Lawrence Levy, and Norman and his caddy, Steve Williams. As they turned off the main road in Hilton

Head and down the last few hundred yards to the air strip, Norman leaned over.

"You're a pretty great kid, Jamie," he said.

The words glowed in Jamie's mind. On the flight home, he turned to his mother. "Mom, he really meant it, didn't he?" he said.

There was another thing that Norman meant. Just before the Huttons boarded the plane, he got Jamie's attention.

"See you at the Open?" he said.

"That's for sure," Jamie said.

The Huttons had no sooner walked into their apartment back home in Monona when the phone rang. It was Norman, making sure they had got home safely. And he wanted to wish Jamie all the best for his trials ahead.

And so what started out as a stricken boy's magic weekend had become magic for a famous golfer, too. For a world made cynical by too many artificial relationships that are exploited for fame and profit, this one was too good to be genuine.

But the cynics were wrong. Day after day, Norman phoned to keep track of Jamie's struggle to survive. Things got rougher for the young man who had suffered so much already.

He had yet another hurdle to overcome. His bone marrow transplant had to be postponed for almost a month because when he got home, he came down with

Ken Venturi of CBS provided a guided tour of the television compound and showed Jamie how the pictures and commentary are sent around the country.

chicken pox. He spent six days in quarantine in the University of Wisconsin hospital. Letters and gifts from well-wishers around the country streamed into his home and hospital room. He received autographed basketballs from Michael Jordan and Larry Bird. And Norman, as he had promised, sent Jamie a set of golf clubs and a golf bag. Each club head was engraved, "To Jamie from Greg."

Doctors found, as expected, that Jamie's brother, Michael, was the best hope for the transfusion of bone marrow. The procedure took place early in June. It is not an easy thing. There is pain, and there are anxious times. Would the transplant "take?" Would Jamie's body accept his brother's gift of life?

There is no easy way to judge a person's real emotions. But there was a moment of truth for Greg Norman. It happened when he was a guest of honor June 7 at the New York Metropolitan Golf Writers Association's annual banquet, held at the time of the Manufacturers Hanover Westchester Classic played at Westchester (New York) Country Club. This banquet would be different.

Earlier in the year, Mary Bea Porter, a member of the Ladies Professional Golf Association Tour and the mother of a young boy, saved the life of a two-year-old child who was drowning in a backyard pool adjacent to the Phoenix, Arizona, golf course where she was competing.

Hearing the cries of family members

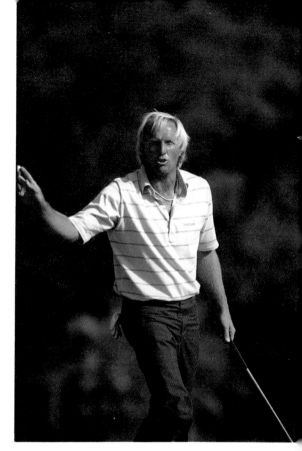

From his position inside the gallery ropes, Jamie watches Greg down the stretch including the all-important birdie at the 15th.

who were almost paralyzed with fright, Mary Bea charged off the fairway, and with the help of her caddy scaled a seven-foot-high fence. She raced to the inert little boy and administered mouth-to-mouth recuscitation.

Members of the Met Golf Writers Association felt that heroic and humanitarian acts such as Mary Bea's and Greg's should be formally recognized. They established the Mary Bea Porter Award, to be given to any golfer — male or female, professional or amateur — who performs such acts. Mary Bea and Greg were the first two recipients.

In a magnificent acceptance speech, Mary Bea pleaded for better knowledge of CPR — cardiopulmonary resuscitation — the emergency skill she had learned long ago and that she used to save the life of that little boy.

Then came Greg Norman's turn to accept his award, and to speak. The people filling the ballroom of the Stamford Sheraton Hotel fell hushed. Norman stepped to the microphone. And nothing came out.

It was an awkward silence. The big guy who had handled so much pressure on the golf course was not prepared for something like this. As he had said earlier, this was not about golf and games. This was about life. Thoughts of Jamie hit him again. He could not get the words out. Tears were streaming down his face. Finally:

"Pardon me," he said. "I've never done this before. Please excuse me."

There wasn't a sound in the hall. Norman fought himself. It was an interminable minute before he was able to speak.

He said he had called Jamie that afternoon, just as he was getting ready for the marrow transplant. The best he could do for Jamie was to hope and pray.

"Jamie spoke of terminal disease with a freedom of expression," he said. "I got whammed with this all of a sudden, as if he had known me for ten years. He was very humble, and accepted the fact that he possibly had a short period of time. And here he is, in great pain and being forced to take drugs to help him get through it.

"This gives me a greater appreciation of what is going on around me, and I am now more anti-drugs than I've ever been before. I can see what this kid is going through. He has to take the drugs, and he doesn't like it. He has to take the drugs to stay alive, and he still doesn't like it.

"I don't think that many people know what goes on with a sick child. Heck, they haven't reached one quarter of their life. They don't have a chance. If ever I see a kid using drugs, I'll go nuts. I don't see why anyone would ruin his or her life. You look at Jamie, who doesn't want to take drugs, and you'll know how I feel."

Mary Bea and Greg received the biggest ovation ever heard at that dinner, where writers have honored such golf heroes as Jack Nicklaus, Arnold Palmer, Ben Hogan, President Eisenhower, Bob Hope, and, on that same evening in 1988, another man who does so much for youngsters, Chi Chi Rodriguez.

Jamie remained in the hospital for a long time. He even had to celebrate his 18th birthday, on September 18, 1988, in a hospital room.

As an inspiration, he just might have made the difference for Norman had he been able to attend the Westchester Classic in June.

One of the tour's dream playoffs went but one extra hole that Sunday. It was Norman, Seve Ballesteros, the wonderfully heroic Spaniard, and David Frost and Ken Green.

Greg had a near-miss at the 16th, but at the 18th the "one for Jamie" was never given the chance to miss. There was, of course, a sigh of relief and an exchange.

Ballesteros won by blasting free of a bunker and getting a birdie-three on the short playoff hole. Norman had made another of those final-round charges, the best round of the tournament, a seven-under-par 64 to catch the others.

The end of the Westchester Classic was only four days before the start of the United States Open at Brookline, Massachusetts. Jamie had said he would see Norman at the Open, but he had to stay in the hospital. His thoughts, though, were with Norman.

And Norman could have used some luck, or whatever it was that Jamie brought him at the Heritage. In the second round, Norman damaged ligaments in his left wrist when his club hit a rock while he was playing the ninth hole. He was forced to withdraw. Worse, the injury put him out of action for about eight weeks.

Curtis Strange won the U.S. Open, beating Nick Faldo of England in an 18-hole playoff. Among his rewards was a letter from Jamie.

"Congratulations," Jamie wrote. "I was rooting so hard for Greg. But after he was hurt and had to leave I was rooting for you."

Strange was pleased, and touched. "The funny thing about that," he said, "is that you know the kid meant exactly that."

Waiting for "the moment" was tense, but when it broke the smiles told the story. Their dream had come true.

The injured wrist forced Norman to pass up the British Open in mid-July, the major championship he had won in 1986, and he was not able to play again until the PGA Championship in Edmond, Oklahoma, the third week in August. But he kept in touch with Jamie at least four times a week, even phoning him when he was on a short trip to Italy.

For a while in July, Norman thought be might be able to play in the British Open. He tried to practice, and found there was too much pain. The kid who had advised him on his putting back at the Heritage Classic now had some even more valuable advice for him.

"Jamie told me in one of our phone conversations," Norman said, " 'Don't do anything foolish. Wait until you're really ready.' "

Not that Norman didn't already know that. But it sounded good coming from the kid whose dream he made come true. They became part of each other's lives that weekend at Hilton Head, and both man and boy were the better for it.

Greg Norman and Jamie Hutton, and everyone around them, had discovered what Henry Thoreau meant.

"Dreams," Thoreau wrote, "are the touchstones of our characters."

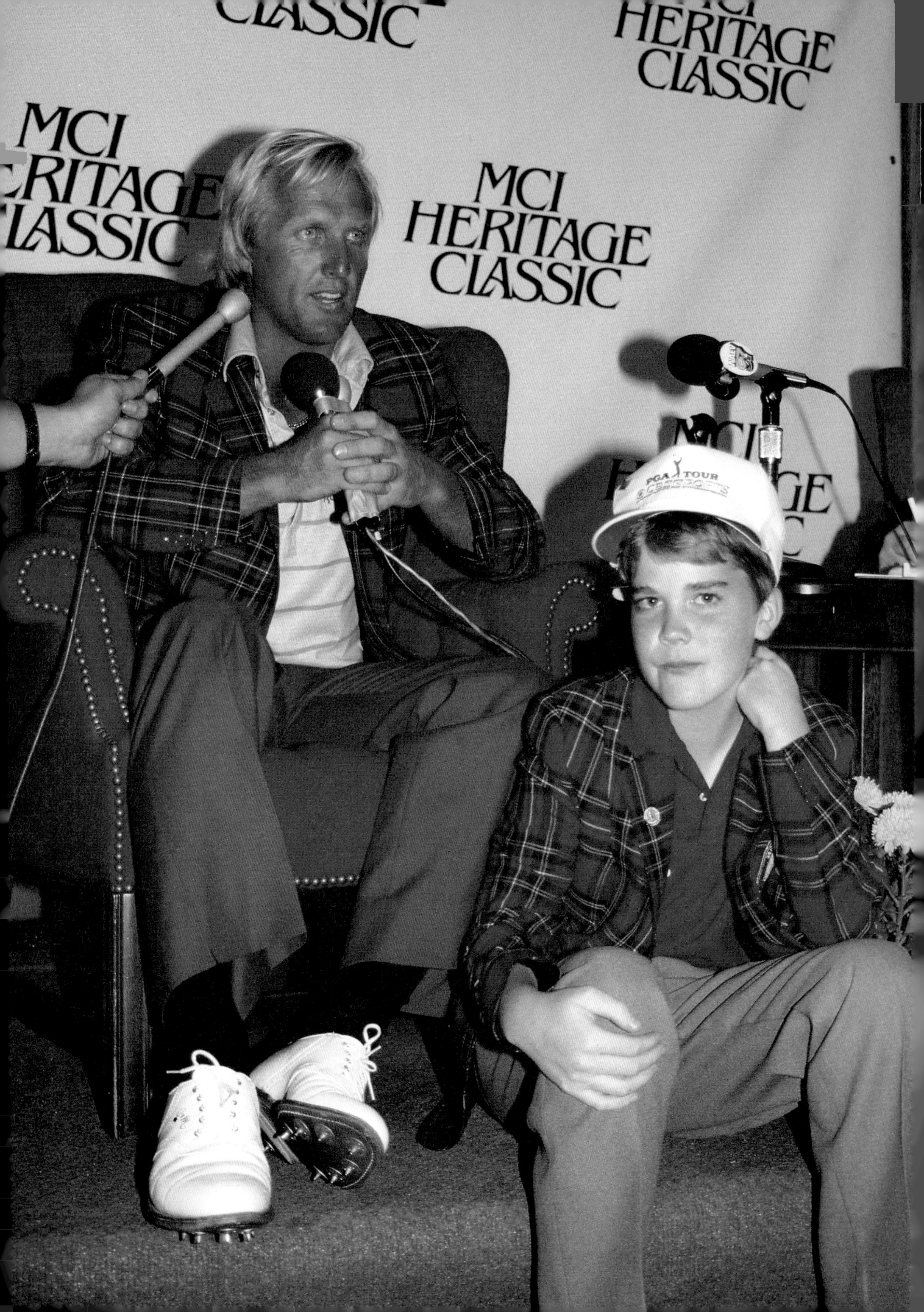
MCI
HERITAGE
CLASSIC
PGA TOUR

Jamie was having the best time of his life, and so was his mother, Garnett (below).

Not goodbye, but farewell, get better. See you soon, and we'll remember this moment for the rest of our lives.